Plate Tectonics and Continental Drift

LOOKING AT LANDSCAPES

Plate Tectonics and Continental Drift

John Edwards

Smart Apple Media

First published in 2005 by Evans Brothers Limited
2A Portman Mansions, Chiltern Street
London W1U 6NR

Consultant: Simon Ross, Editor: Sonya Newland, Designer: Big Blu Ltd.,
Picture Researcher: Julia Bird

Published in the United States by Smart Apple Media
2140 Howard Drive West, North Mankato, Minnesota 56003

Library of Congress Cataloging-in-Publication Data

Edwards, John.
Plate tectonics and continental drift / by John Edwards.
p. cm. — (Looking at landscapes)
Includes index.
ISBN 1-58340-730-8
1. Plate tectonics—Juvenile literature. 2. Continental drift—Juvenile literature. I. Title. II. Series.

QE511.4.E29 2005
551.1'36—dc22   2005043056

9 8 7 6 5 4 3 2 1

Contents

Introduction

Scientists believe that, millions of years ago, all of the land on Earth was joined together in one large mass surrounded by a single, vast ocean. Eventually, this land mass broke apart, the pieces started to move away from one another, and oceans formed between them. They eventually formed the continents that we know today. This movement is still happening—the continents are drifting, sometimes breaking apart, sometimes shifting closer together. They move very slowly, between one-third and four inches (1–10 cm) per year.

The reason for the movement of the continents lies deep beneath the oceans. Earth's entire surface is actually made up of a number of huge slabs called tectonic plates, which are in constant motion. They move very slowly, but their sheer size means that if these plates bump into, pull away from, or grind past one another, the effects can be dramatic. Many strange but impressive features are formed as a result of plate movement: strings of volcanic islands in the middle of the ocean, chains of underwater mountain ranges, and great trenches in the ocean floor—the very deepest and darkest places on our planet.

The movement of Earth's plates can cause volcanic islands to form. This one lies off the coast of Iceland. The craters appear when hot gases bubble up through the lava when the island is being formed.

Plate movement itself is caused by activity deep inside Earth. Earth's solid inner core is radioactive, which generates forces that move the softer rock in the layers above it. Temperature and pressure here are very high, so the molten rock just beneath Earth's surface "flows," causing the plates on top of it to inch slowly but constantly in different directions.

Many of the effects of tectonic movement do not directly affect us—the processes happen so slowly that they are almost imperceptible. However, two of the most familiar consequences of plate movement can have serious effects on human life: earthquakes and volcanic eruptions. These have been occurring for millions of years and still happen frequently. Most earthquakes are so small that they go largely unnoticed, but some can be huge, and when they occur in populated areas, they can cause devastation to property and loss of life. Volcanoes are also created by tectonic movement and can be equally devastating. Although most of the world's volcanoes are extinct or dormant, more than 1,000 are active. When they erupt, they can spew out rivers of boiling, molten lava and clouds of hot dust, ash, and rock. These can travel for many miles, destroying the surrounding land and covering whole cities with layers of suffocating ash.

Despite these dangers, the movement of Earth's plates has created some of the most beautiful and dramatic landscapes on Earth—and will continue to do so for many millions of years to come. In the far distant future, the features of Earth and the position of the continents and oceans that are so familiar to us now will be very different.

▲ This fissure in the floor of the ocean—at a depth of around 8,530 feet (2,600 m)—was caused by tectonic plates pulling apart from each other. As the plates spread, Earth's crust is stretched, and cracks form.

The Structure of Earth

The Earth is probably about five billion years old. In the beginning, it would have been a boiling mass of molten rock and gas. So much heat was given off that today, millions of years later, the temperature at Earth's center is around 11,200 °F (6,200 °C). Our planet is still cooling down.

As Earth began to cool, different materials started to separate. More dense materials, such as iron, formed Earth's core. Lighter materials, such as silicates, floated to the surface. Distinct layers began to form inside the planet.

Presently, Earth is made up of these layers. The surface or outer layer is called the crust and is divided into sections called plates. The crust is very thin compared with the size of Earth—on average, only 12 miles (20 km) in depth. If Earth was the size of a soccer ball, the crust would be less than .04 inch (1 mm) thick. The thickest and oldest crust is the continental crust, the outer layer of Earth, which is, on average, 22 miles (35 km) deep. Continental crust is dominated by crystalline rocks rich in quartz and feldspar. Some of these rocks are 3.5 billion years old. Oceanic crust is much thinner and younger, averaging only 4 miles (6 km) thick and about 200 million years old. Oceanic crust is

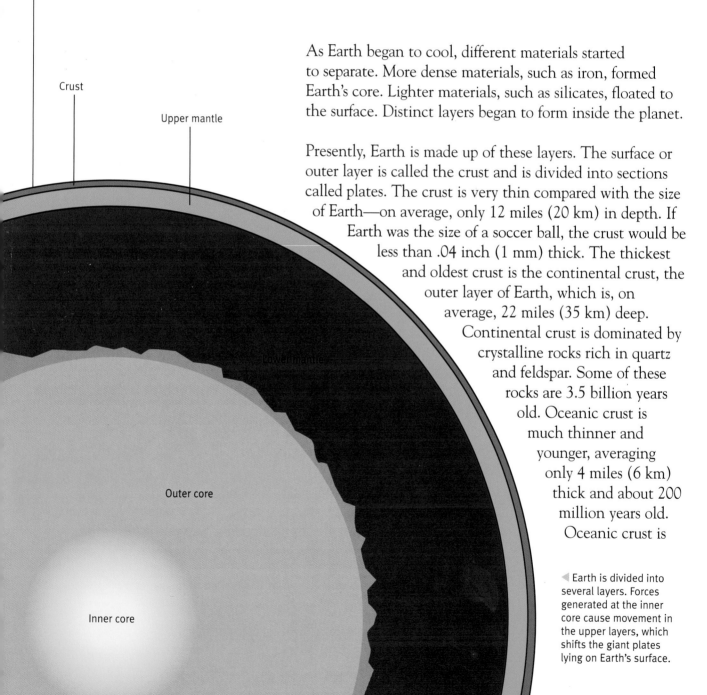

Crust

Upper mantle

Lower mantle

Outer core

Inner core

◀ Earth is divided into several layers. Forces generated at the inner core cause movement in the upper layers, which shifts the giant plates lying on Earth's surface.

largely made up of a dense rock called basalt, formed by a network of underwater volcanoes. New crust is being formed all the time.

▲ A chain of underwater volcanoes—known as the Three Wise Men—situated in the South Pacific Ocean. These are part of a string of volcanoes more than 25,000 miles (40,000 km) long, which stretches around the world and is constantly creating new oceanic crust.

The broken Earth

The zone of rock below the crust is called the mantle. This is nearly 1,865 miles (3,000 km) thick and is made mostly of iron and magnesium. The mantle is divided into several layers. The upper part is solid rock, but at greater depths, it becomes molten. Rocks in the mantle are continually on the move. This movement is the root cause of the world's earthquakes and volcanoes.

The layer beneath the mantle is the core. The outer core is made of iron and nickel, which is so hot that it remains in a liquid state. The center of Earth is the inner core. Although the inner core is also made of iron and nickel and is extremely hot, it remains solid because the rocks are under so much pressure that they are pressed together.

Earth can be compared to a hard-boiled egg. The yolk represents the core, the white the mantle, and the shell the crust. If the egg is knocked on a hard surface, the shell cracks, but all the pieces stay in position. Earth's plates fit together like a jigsaw puzzle.

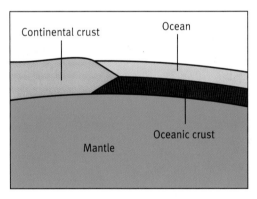

Continental crust

Ocean

Oceanic crust

Mantle

▲ Both continental and oceanic crust lie just above Earth's mantle. Oceanic crust is covered by the seas. Continental crust rises above the ocean.

The lithosphere

The rigid shell of Earth is called the lithosphere, from the Greek word *lithos*, meaning "stone." Instead of being smooth, it is broken into massive fragments. These fragments are called tectonic plates or, sometimes, lithospheric plates.

The Theory of Plate Tectonics

The crust is Earth's rocky outer shell. It is not continuous over the entire surface of the planet but is actually broken into huge areas called tectonic plates, which lie on top of Earth's mantle.

The plates are made up of solid rock, which ranges from 4 to 40 miles (6.5–65 km) thick. Tectonic plates vary in shape and size—there are nine large plates, as well as several smaller ones. Tectonic plates are not defined by continents or oceans; they can cut through them, as the map below shows. However, six of the nine large plates are named after the continents that lie within them: North

▼ Some of the plates that make up Earth's surface are moving apart, while others are colliding. This map shows the various plates and the directions of their movement.

American, South American, Eurasian, African, Indo-Australian, and Antarctic. The Pacific, Nazca, and Cocos plates are oceanic—they contain oceans instead of continents. The other plates shown might be much smaller, but their movement can have the same effects as the large plates, and they are capable of causing just as much damage on Earth's surface.

How do we know about plate movement?

Tectonic plates are constantly moving. The North American and African plates, for example, are moving apart, while the Eurasian and African plates are colliding. The average rate of movement is between one-third and four inches (1–10 cm) per year. Earth's plates are moving at about the speed at which your fingernails grow. Plate movement is so slow that we cannot feel it happening, so what first gave people the idea that Earth was made up of gigantic plates? And how did they find out how they moved around?

During the 19th century, scientists began to look at the shape of the different land masses on Earth. They noticed that the east coast of South America seemed to fit together with the west coast of Africa like puzzle pieces. German scientist Alfred Wegener (1880–1930) suggested that perhaps these continents had once been joined together. If this was the case, then it was likely that all the continents had once formed a single large land mass. Over time, this land mass broke up, and the continents floated on the ocean floor to the positions they are in today.

▲ This image of Earth from space shows the phenomenon that scientists in the 19th century began to wonder about—the shape of the east coast of South America (center left) seems to fit with the shape of the west coast of Africa (upper right) like pieces in a puzzle.

◀ Alfred Wegener, the German scientist who first proposed the theory of continental drift. Although evidence seemed to prove his theory, Wegener was unable to explain exactly how such massive pieces of land had broken apart and moved around, and for many years, his ideas were not taken seriously.

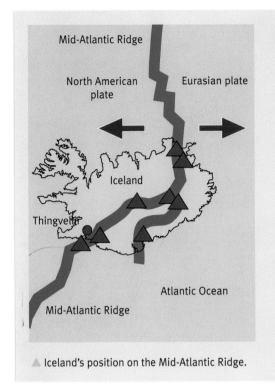

Iceland's position on the Mid-Atlantic Ridge.

🌑 Iceland—land of fire and ice

Geologically, Iceland is one of the youngest countries in the world. No part of Iceland is more than 20 million years old. It is situated on the Mid-Atlantic Ridge, where the Eurasian and North American plates are tearing apart. This means that volcanic eruptions are a constant threat. Since the island was first inhabited in the ninth century, there have been more than 150 recorded volcanic eruptions. These eruptions also create new land, such as the Westman Islands off the south coast of the mainland.

The rift between the two plates is visible at several locations in Iceland. At Thingvellir in the southwest, scientists have watched and measured the continents of Europe and America separating at a rate of almost a quarter inch (5 mm) per year. In the last century, the trench has grown by approximately 20 inches (50 cm). This is the narrowest gap between the two plates anywhere along the ridge.

In addition to the shape of South America and Africa, Wegener used evidence from the rocks in these regions to support his theory. The mountains running across South Africa seemed to link to those in Argentina in South America. Also, in his studies of layers of rock sequences, Wegener discovered that the lower layers—and therefore the oldest—were the same on both sides of the Atlantic Ocean, which divides the two land masses. Wegener suggested that these ancient layers were made when the continents were part of a single land mass. Fossilized plant species were also common across both regions. Many of these organisms could not possibly have traveled across the oceans that now separate the different continents.

Despite this evidence, Wegener's ideas were not generally accepted at the time. It was not until the 1960s that new evidence was found to support the theory of continental drift. By this time, scientists had a much better understanding of what happened on the ocean floors. It was clear that new ocean crust was continually being created, which, in turn, helped to drive the movement of the continents. Wegener's original theory was put together with newer ideas to form the overall theory we now know as plate tectonics.

◀◀ The huge crack in the ground (left of center) is part of the Mid-Atlantic Ridge at Thingvellir in Iceland. This is one of the only places in the world where the ridge can be seen on the surface of Earth. Almost everywhere else, mid-ocean ridges are deep below the water.

⊕ Oceanic and continental plates

Oceanic plates are large slabs of oceanic or continental crust. They are composed of a heavy rock called basalt, so they tend to sink deeper into Earth's mantle.

Continental plates are made of granite, which is much lighter than basalt, so these plates tend to rise and float above the oceanic plates. They are also much thinner than the oceanic plates.

▶▶ In 1963, a completely new island emerged from the sea south of the Icelandic mainland. It was named Surtsey, after Surtr, a fire giant from Norwegian mythology. The creation of islands such as Surtsey is just one consequence of plate movement.

▼ Scientists believe that the movement of Earth's plates is driven by convection currents in the mantle.

Why is Earth's surface moving?

What causes plates the size of a continent to move? Many scientists believe that it is heat from within Earth that powers the movement of the plates on its surface. At temperatures of more than 1,800 °F (1,000 °C), the rocks in the mantle near the core melt and start to flow toward the surface. The high pressure of rocks in the crust above stops them from melting in the heat. Nearer the surface, the rocks cool, flow sideways, and then return toward the core. It is believed that the rocks in Earth's mantle form giant convection currents.

The sideways (lateral) movement of rocks just beneath the crust causes the plates on the surface to move. When two currents move toward each other, the plates riding on them move as well; when two currents separate, so do the plates. This important difference results in the various types of plate boundaries. The plates move at different speeds and in different directions. Although most of them only move as little as one-third of an inch (1 cm) per year, over millions of years, this movement has completely changed the pattern of land and sea on Earth's surface. It is still changing.

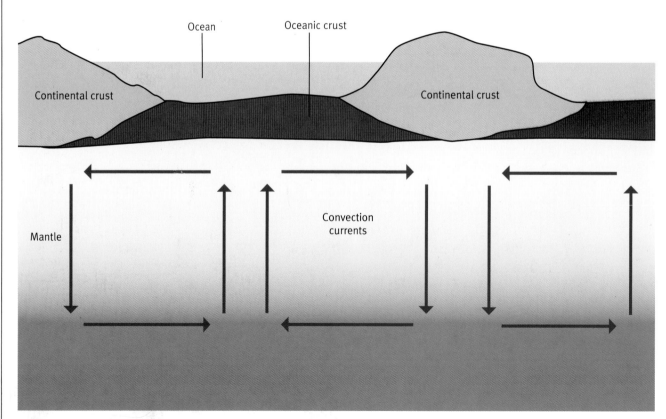

Ocean

Oceanic crust

Continental crust

Continental crust

Mantle

Convection currents

Continental Drift

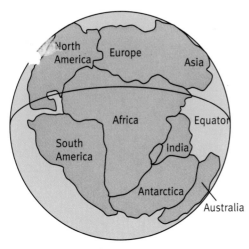

▲ The super-continent of Pangaea.

According to the theory of plate tectonics, all of the continents were once joined together in a single, vast land mass. This huge super-continent, called Pangaea, was surrounded by a giant ocean called Panthalassa. The diagrams on the left show the positions of present-day continents within Pangaea. Notice how little Africa has altered in all this time, but how far India has to travel before it becomes a part of Asia. Scientists believe that this land mass began to break up approximately 200 million years ago as a result of the same processes that are at work today.

At first, Pangaea broke into two new continents called Laurasia and Gondwanaland. Europe, Asia, and North America were all joined together as Laurasia. Gondwanaland was made up of Africa, Australia, South America, and Antarctica. Until 150 million years ago, India remained a part of this land mass.

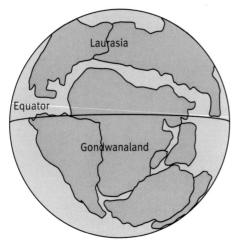

▲ The development and breakup of Laurasia and Gondwanaland.

After Laurasia and Gondwanaland broke apart, the continental land masses started to drift farther. By 130 million years ago, the continents had begun to take the shapes that we are familiar with today. The Atlantic Ocean started to form as Europe and North America drifted apart. Antarctica was moving south toward its current frozen climate—and India was on its way to crash into Asia.

🌑 A topsy-turvy world

Because of the movement of the continents, countries and places we know today were once in very different positions across the globe. The equator would once have cut through North America, and at one time, the Sahara Desert in Africa was positioned at the South Pole.

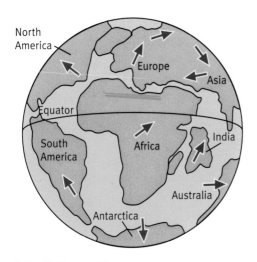

▲ The Earth 130 million years ago.

▶ The movement of the continents at the present time.

North America

Europe

Asia

Africa

Equator

India

South America

Australia

Antarctica

What is happening today?

The arrows on the map show the directions in which the continents are currently moving. Europe and North America continue to drift farther apart, making the Atlantic Ocean larger. Britain and the United States are moving farther away from each other at a rate of around three-quarters of an inch (2 cm) a year. North and South America have joined, and Australia is moving northward. India has at last completed its journey north and plowed into Asia, creating the world's highest range of mountains, the Himalayas.

▷ The fossil of this long-extinct fish was found in the cliffs above Chaleur Bay in the Gaspe Peninsula in Canada. When it was alive, it would have been swimming in seas close to the equator. However, the movement of Earth's plates over millions of years has resulted in this bay being relocated to an extreme northern latitude.

🌑 The traveling continents

The continents have moved huge distances over the many millions of years of Earth's history. In the distant future, America may have drifted so far to the west that it will collide with Asia, and the Pacific Ocean will disappear altogether.

If the drift of the continents continues at its current rate, how will the world look in the future? The map below shows what Earth's surface could look like 50 million years from now. Australia will be much farther north than it is now. North and South America will be separated, and Africa, turning clockwise, will have collided with Europe. However, we can only guess at what will happen this far in the future—nothing is certain. The surface of Earth is in constant motion, shaping landforms and affecting people throughout the world. Even after all of the land masses have collided and converged in the distant future, they will start to break up once again, and will continue to do so forever on this slow-moving but inevitable cycle.

▷ The world 50 million years from now.

▷▷ The high, jagged peaks of the Himalayan mountain range were caused by the collision of the plates carrying India and Asia millions of years ago. The Indian plate was made of solid rock, whereas the Asian plate was formed from softer, sedimentary rock. As the plates collided, the softer rock on the edge of the Asian plate was forced upward, creating mountains. Continuing plate movement in this region means that the Himalayas are still growing.

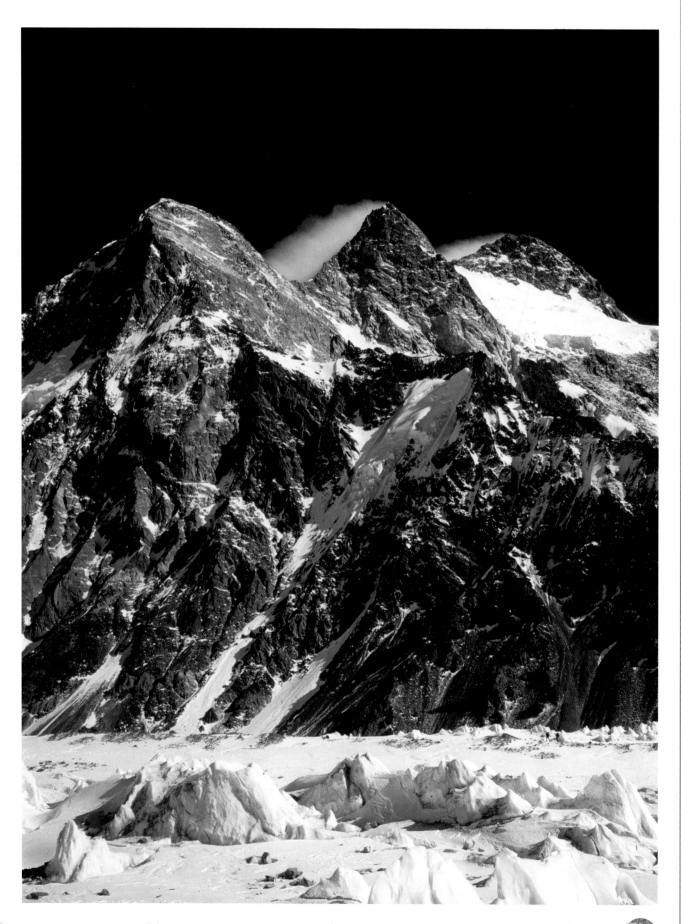

Plate Margins

Earth's plates may move very slowly in human terms, but this movement is responsible for some of the most spectacular landscapes—and some of the most dangerous hazards—on our planet. These processes take place at the edges, or boundaries, of these plates, where two or more of them meet. The movement of convection currents in Earth causes three different types of plate boundaries, depending on the movement of the plates:

▲ This black smoke is coming from an underwater vent in the Mid-Atlantic Ridge, where volcanic liquid is bubbling up through Earth's crust.

- **Divergent** (constructive) boundary. This is where plates move apart.
- **Convergent** (destructive) boundary. This is where plates collide.
- **Transform** (conservative) boundary. This is where plates slide horizontally past one another.

At each of these boundaries, or plate margins, the type of movement causes different phenomena and can even change the face of Earth itself. Even though some plates seem to be moving independently of others, they are all connected. The movement of one plate can affect another one, even if it is thousands of miles away.

Divergent boundaries and mid-ocean ridges

Divergent boundaries occur where two plates move away from each other. They are pushed apart by molten rock, or magma, rising from the mantle beneath the crust. As soon as the magma reaches the surface, it solidifies, forming new crust. This is why this type of plate boundary is sometimes called a constructive boundary.

▶ This sonograph image shows the Reykjanes Ridge, part of the Mid-Atlantic Ridge that lies south of Iceland. The lighter areas are lava that has hardened and formed hills and hummocks (seen most clearly at lower left).

One of the most significant effects of plates moving apart in this way is the formation of mid-ocean ridges. As their name suggests, mid-ocean ridges run along the bottom of the world's oceans at the boundaries of two plates pulling apart. They are essentially long chains of underwater mountains, stretching around 40,000 miles (65,000 km) through Earth's oceans. Some of the mountains in the mid-ocean ridges are more than 11,500 feet (3,500 m) high. The ridges are caused by magma solidifying to fill the cracks caused by the divergent plates separating. The magma cools and attaches to the edge of the plates, where it literally renews the "floor" of Earth. This process is called seafloor spreading. All plates have a "leading edge"—the front of the plate as it is moving away—and a "trailing edge"—the part at the back. The new crust is formed at the trailing edge, so the closer to the leading edge the crust is, the older it is. Mid-ocean ridges are where much of the immense heat from inside Earth is released.

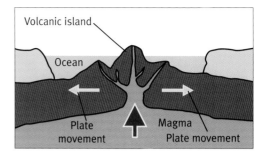

▲ In a divergent plate boundary, two plates move away from each other. Volcanic islands can be formed at divergent boundaries as magma forces its way up through cracks between the plates.

▼ Mid-ocean ridges stretch across the seafloors around the world, formed by plates pulling away from each other. The locations of the ridges are shown on the map below.

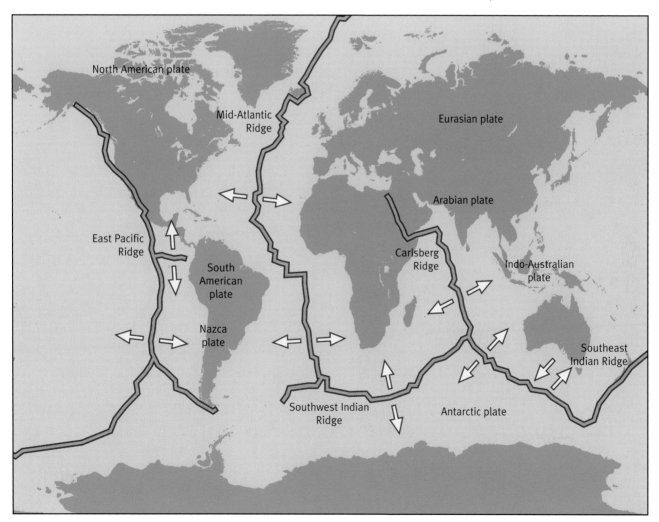

North American plate

Mid-Atlantic Ridge

Eurasian plate

Arabian plate

East Pacific Ridge

South American plate

Carlsberg Ridge

Indo-Australian plate

Nazca plate

Southeast Indian Ridge

Southwest Indian Ridge

Antarctic plate

🌐 The Mid-Atlantic Ridge

Perhaps the best known mid-ocean ridge is the Mid-Atlantic Ridge. This extends from the Arctic Ocean to beyond South Africa. Over the last 200 million years, the North American and Eurasian plates have been pushing apart at the Mid-Atlantic Ridge; this has created the Atlantic Ocean, which is still growing at barely more than three-quarters of an inch (2 cm) every year. Most of the Mid-Atlantic Ridge is below sea level, with the exception of the island of Iceland.

▷ Congealed lava on the Mid-Atlantic Ridge. The lava has been pushed up from Earth's mantle and then cooled and hardened by the ocean.

Where oceanic and continental plates collide

Convergent boundaries occur where two or more plates collide. The type of collision depends on the nature of the plates involved.

The Nazca plate to the west of South America is an oceanic plate (see page 10). It is colliding with the South American plate, which is a continental plate. As it does so, the Nazca plate is forced underneath the South American plate. The area where this happens is called a subduction zone, and because Earth's crust can be destroyed here, this type of boundary is sometimes called a destructive plate boundary. As plates meet, a deep trench forms at the bottom of the sea. These ocean trenches form the deepest parts of the oceans. The Peru-Chile trench runs for thousands of miles along the eastern Pacific Ocean where the Nazca and South American plates meet. It ranges from 5 to 6 miles (8–10 km) in depth. As the oceanic plate subducts, some of the sediment from the ocean floor is scraped off and joined to the leading edge of the continental plate on top. Scientists think this may be why the Andes mountains still seem to be growing—as the Nazca plate dives into the Peru-Chile trench, sediment builds beneath the mountains, forcing them upward.

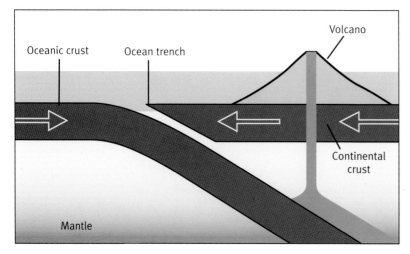

Oceanic crust Ocean trench

Volcano

Continental crust

Mantle

At destructive boundaries, where oceanic and continental plates meet, the oceanic plate can be forced beneath the continental plate, forming a subduction zone. Ocean trenches, earthquakes, and volcanoes are all features of destructive boundaries.

As the oceanic plate is forced downward, violent collisions take place between the two plates. These are earthquakes. When the crust continues descending, it melts due to friction and the higher temperatures that exist in Earth's mantle. The melting crust forms magma. Some of this newly formed magma rises to the surface in the form of volcanoes.

The Andes mountains were formed by the subduction of the Nazca plate under the South American plate. Scientists believe that the Andes are getting higher as the plate movement continues in this way.

Trench-flipping

The collision of an oceanic and a continental plate can also cause a phenomenon called trench-flipping. The continental material cannot sink, so it moves into a trench, where it gets stuck. Its leading edge is squished or folded into mountains. This in turn causes some of the oceanic crust to sit on top of the continental material. Pressure in this region grows until it forces the trench to "flip"—the oceanic plate moves back under the continental crust.

Eventually, two continents will crash into each other. When this happens, the trench disappears and new mountain ranges are formed. It is possible for a plate to disappear altogether, but this would only occur if a plate was diving into a subduction trench more quickly than the new crust was being formed at the trailing edge. This could have dramatic consequences, though, as the disappearance of a whole plate would change the position of all others on Earth.

▼ This sonar image shows an area of subduction on the floor of the Pacific Ocean off the coast of North America, where the Juan de Fuca plate is being pushed down by the North American plate. This causes sediments to build up into the ridges seen along the middle of the image. The colors represent the depth of the ocean: orange is 3,280 feet (1,000 m), yellow is 6,560 feet (2,000 m), and green is 9,840 feet (3,000 m).

Challenger Deep

The Pacific and Philippine plates are two colliding oceanic plates. The Marianas Trench marks the location where the two plates meet. Challenger Deep is at the southern end of the Marianas Trench. It is the lowest part of any ocean, reaching nearly seven miles (11 km) below sea level.

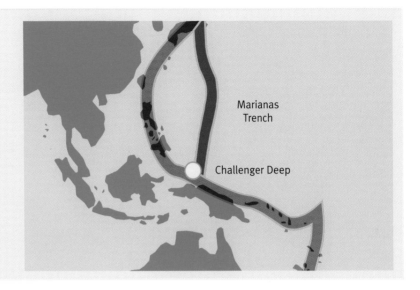

▶ Challenger Deep is the lowest part of any ocean on Earth.

Where ocean plates collide

Where two oceanic plates meet, one is usually pushed underneath the other, and the processes involved are the same as when oceanic and continental plates meet. As the plates collide, the younger plate will move over the older plate because it is less dense. The older plate bends under the pressure and is forced deeper into Earth, forming a huge trench. As the plate descends, it can trigger earthquakes that can affect continents, even though they are caused by oceanic plates.

◀ A computer model showing the region surrounding the Marianas Trench in the Pacific Ocean. The depth of the ocean is color coded: dark green areas are land, pink areas are nearest to the surface, then yellow, green, and blue. The deepest point—the trench itself—is colored purple.

▲ This is a satellite image of the Aleutian Islands in Alaska, forming an island arc. They lie at the northern edge of the Pacific Ring of Fire.

The descending plate heats up, and, at great depths, the rock begins to melt, forming magma. The magma begins the return journey, rising toward the surface. It bubbles up at the leading edge, cools down, and attaches to the crust, forming volcanoes. These grow bigger as the process continues, until they are so high that they rise above the surface of the water, forming a string of volcanic islands called an island arc. The islands of the Caribbean and the Aleutian Islands were formed in this way.

🌐 The Pacific Ring of Fire

The Ring of Fire is the name given to the most famous island arc—the huge chain of volcanoes surrounding the Pacific Ocean. It gets its name from the frequency of active volcanoes and from the large number of volcanoes that have not recently erupted (dormant volcanoes). Three-quarters of the world's volcanoes can be found here. The Ring of Fire extends from South America to North America, to Japan, then down to New Zealand.

▶ The ocean trenches surrounding the Pacific Ring of Fire.

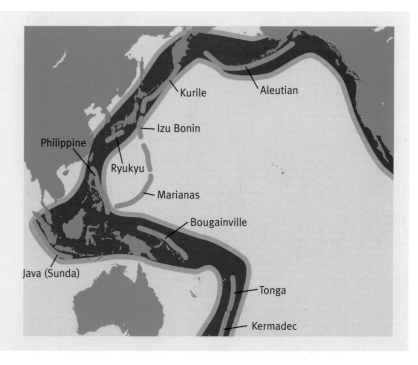

🌍 The Himalayan mountains

The Indo-Australian plate collided with the Eurasian plate 50 million years ago. It is still moving north at a rate of two inches (5 cm) per year. The boundary between the two plates was buckled and forced upward, forming the Himalayan mountains—the highest mountain range on Earth. As the plates continue to collide, the world's highest mountains are getting higher.

▶ Mount Everest in the Himalayas is the highest mountain in the world. As the two plates collide, it is still gaining height.

Where continental plates collide

Scientists once believed that mountains were formed millions of years ago when Earth was very young. They thought that the planet had once been a molten ball and that, as it cooled down, its surface cracked and folded up on itself, throwing up the peaks of the world's mountain ranges. Later, as their understanding of Earth grew, scientists realized that this theory did not quite work; it would mean that all of the mountain ranges would be roughly the same age, and they knew this was not the case. Today, we known that mountains are a result of the collision between two continental plates.

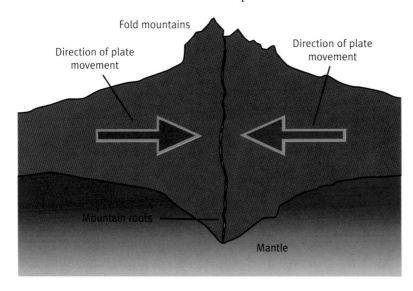

Fold mountains

Direction of plate movement

Direction of plate movement

Mountain roots

Mantle

◀ The collision of two continental plates forces huge amounts of rock upward. After many thousands of years, these build into mountain ranges such as the Himalayas; they are called fold mountains because the earth "folded" upward to form them.

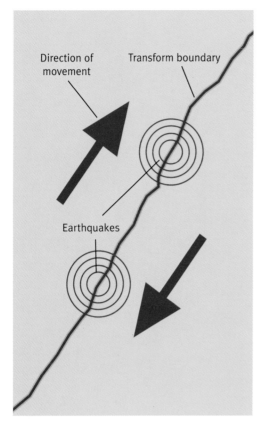

Earthquakes occur at transform plate boundaries, where two plates are grinding against each other.

A seismologist (a scientist who studies earthquakes) investigates an area of earthquake activity. The cracks in the earth are still steaming.

Emergency services at work after the earthquake in San Francisco in October 1989. The city lies on the San Andreas Fault and is subject to many earthquakes caused by plate movement.

When two continental plates meet, neither plate is pushed downward (subducted). Instead, they collide and are buckled upward, creating fold mountains. When the two plates meet, enormous piles of crumpled rock are forced upward to build up on Earth's surface. Over many years, the rocks are weathered to form the jagged peaks we associate with mountains today. The Himalayas and the Andes mountain ranges were formed in this way. Although they appear to be very old, these mountains were only formed in the last 50 million years and are therefore relatively young in terms of Earth's long history.

Transform boundaries and faults

Not all of Earth's plates are moving apart or crashing into one another. Some plates slide horizontally against each other at transform boundaries. No crust is created or destroyed at these boundaries, which is why they are sometimes called "conservative" plate boundaries. This means that there are no volcanoes. However, the movement of these giant plates releases enormous amounts of energy, as the plates tend to stick, then slip violently, rather than sliding smoothly against each other. The movement at transform boundaries can cause fractures in Earth's crust, called faults. Fold mountains and earthquakes are common features of faults.

The San Andreas Fault

The San Andreas Fault marks the boundary between the Pacific and North American plates. Both plates are moving in a northwesterly direction, but the Pacific plate moves more quickly—two inches (6 cm) per year, compared with the North American plate's one-third inch (1 cm). The San Andreas Fault is more than 800 miles (1,300 km) long. The plates do not slide easily against each other, and earthquakes occur when there is sudden movement. Since this area of the U.S. is heavily populated, these earthquakes can cause severe disruption and loss of life. A major earthquake could happen at any time along the San Andreas Fault. If the present movement of the plates continues, Los Angeles will someday be north of San Francisco.

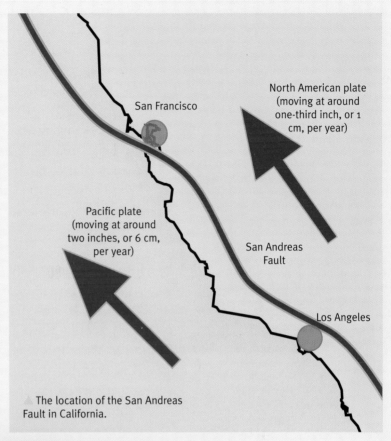

San Francisco

North American plate (moving at around one-third inch, or 1 cm, per year)

Pacific plate (moving at around two inches, or 6 cm, per year)

San Andreas Fault

Los Angeles

The location of the San Andreas Fault in California.

Plate boundary zones

Not every plate boundary fits easily into one of these categories. Some are so complicated that it is difficult to know the exact location of the boundary. Scientists have determined the approximate location of the plate boundaries through charting phenomena such as earthquakes and volcanoes, and have figured out where most activity takes place. The effects of plate movements can also extend over a large area, not just where the two plates meet. In these situations, there is a plate boundary zone. An example of such a zone is the Mediterranean region of Europe, where the African and Eurasian plates meet. The volcanoes and earthquakes in Italy are caused by the meeting of the two plates in this zone.

Rifts and hot spots

Activity related to Earth's tectonic plates can even happen away from the boundaries. Sometimes, a plate carrying a continent can actually split apart. This happens when

▲ Lava erupts from the Stromboli volcano in Italy. Activity in this region occurs at a plate boundary zone where the exact location of the meeting plates is unknown.

🌐 The Great Rift Valley

The Great Rift Valley is the most famous example of a rift in Earth caused by tectonic movement. It stretches for 1,865 miles (3,000 km) along East Africa. The valley ranges from nearly 1,312 feet (400 m) below sea level to nearly 6,560 feet (2,000 m) above sea level, and has many lakes, rivers, and high, jagged cliffs along its course. Because it was formed through the weakening of Earth's crust by magma beneath its surface, the area of the Great Rift Valley is volcanically active. Mount Kilimanjaro—the highest point in Africa—is probably the best-known volcanic mountain in the region, although it is believed to be extinct.

▶ The Great Rift Valley running through central Kenya in Africa.

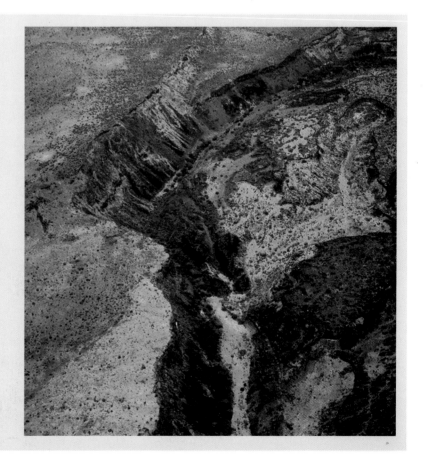

Mountains on Mars

As technology allows us to see the other planets in our solar system in increasing detail, scientists have begun to wonder whether plate activity might be at work elsewhere in the universe. There are many features on Mars, for example, that are similar to those on the surface of Earth. Among these are craters, rifts, and volcanoes.

Volcanic eruptions have also been seen on Jupiter's moons, and the landscape of Venus is characterized by lava plains.

▼ Olympus Mons is the largest known volcano in the solar system. Situated on Mars, it rises 17 miles (27 km) above the surrounding land (Mount Everest is only 5.5 miles, or 8.8 km, high). Has plate movement beneath the surface of the planet caused this?

▶▶ Fountains of lava spewing from Mauna Loa—one of five active volcanoes on the main Hawaiian island.

▶ Lava can flow at speeds of up to 30 miles (50 km) per hour from volcanoes like Kilauea, on the Pacific hot spot.

▽ The Hawaiian islands as seen from space. This chain of islands in the Pacific Ocean is formed by a series of volcanoes moving over a hot spot in Earth's crust.

magma builds up toward continental crust, making it weaker and eventually causing it to crack. Parts of the crust drop, forming an immense rift valley. These valleys are actually ocean basins—the first stage in the formation of a new ocean and, eventually, a new tectonic plate. Over a long period of time, the sea will fill the rift. As this happens, the rift—now under the water—will develop a lava ridge of mountains. All of the mid-ocean ridges began with the creation of a series of rift valleys.

Although most of Earth's volcanoes lie at the edge of tectonic plates, there are some that are situated a long way from these boundaries. These are called intraplate volcanoes. Most of these volcanoes are dormant, but several are still active—the most famous of these are Mauna Loa and Kilauea on the Hawaiian islands in the Pacific Ocean. They exist because they are situated over hot spots. A hot spot is a huge fountain of lava beneath Earth's surface, which burns through crust that is thinner than normal to form a volcano. The lava fountain always stays in the same place, but as the plate moves above it, the existing volcanoes are moved away from the hot spot, and new volcanoes are formed. In Hawaii, there is a string of dead volcanoes like this—each one was formed by sitting over the hot spot and has now been moved on by plate movement. The active volcanoes are the ones currently over the hot spot.

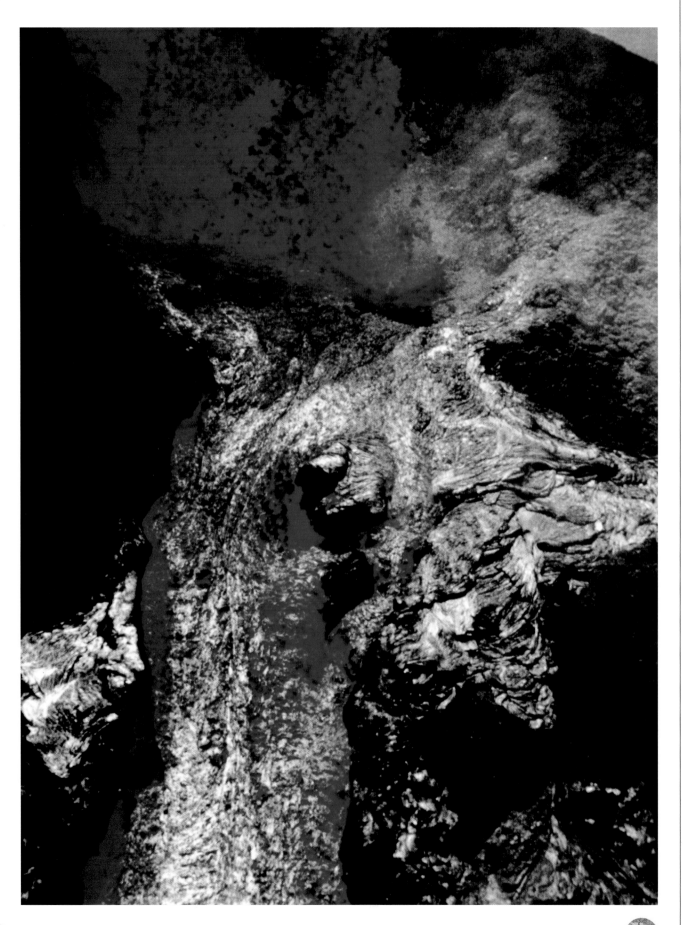

The Hazards Caused by Plate Movements

Although the movements of plates and continents are imperceptible to us, over many years, these processes have created some of the most spectacular scenery in the world. However, these same movements can also cause some serious hazards. Two of the most destructive of these are earthquakes and volcanic eruptions.

The understanding scientists now have of plate tectonics helps to explain the location of earthquakes and volcanoes. Earthquakes occur only in narrow belts across Earth; there are similar zones of activity for volcanoes. It is at the plate boundaries, where plates are moving together or spreading apart, that earthquakes and volcanic eruptions occur.

▼ The concentration of earthquake activity around the world. It is clear from the map that earthquakes occur in "belts" around plate margins.

ZONES OF EARTHQUAKE ACTIVITY AROUND THE WORLD

Recorded earthquake

Earthquake zones

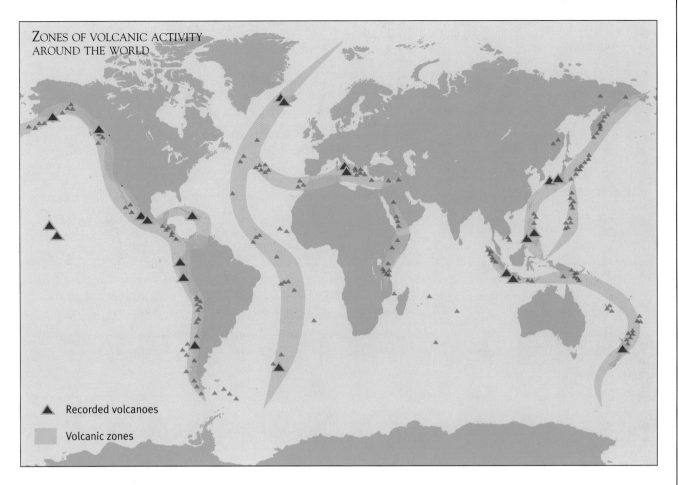

ZONES OF VOLCANIC ACTIVITY AROUND THE WORLD

▲ Recorded volcanoes

▨ Volcanic zones

What is an earthquake?

An earthquake is a sudden release of energy in Earth's crust or the upper part of the mantle. Earthquakes usually occur when two plates moving in different directions become stuck, and then the pressure is suddenly released.

The actual location of an earthquake is often underground. This location is called the focus. The place on Earth's surface directly above this is called the epicenter. If the focus is near the surface, an earthquake is likely to cause more damage than if it is located far underground.

▲ Volcanic zones also lie around plate margins, although they are concentrated in fewer regions than earthquake activity. The Hawaiian islands in the Pacific Ocean are formed from volcanoes such as Mauna Loa and Kilauea.

▽ An earthquake is caused when parts of two plates sliding past each other get stuck. Enormous tension builds up, and eventually rock gives way. The tension is released in the form of energy, or seismic waves, which send out vibrations in all directions.

Plates try to move, but stick

Sudden movement as plates pull apart

Sudden movement causes seismic waves

Epicenter

Focus

🌑 Tsunamis

Tsunamis are huge waves of water caused by the sudden vertical movement of the seafloor during an earthquake. They can also be caused by volcanic eruptions or landslides beneath the sea. In the deep ocean, the height of a tsunami is usually no more than three feet (1 m), but the waves can travel at more than 400 miles (650 km) per hour. As tsunamis reach shallow water, they slow down, and the height of the waves increases dramatically, sometimes reaching 80 feet (25 m). The earthquake responsible for the series of tsunamis across Asia in December 2004 was caused when the Indian plate slipped beneath the Eurasian plate. The seafloor was thrust upward, creating massive amounts of energy that sent giant waves racing across the Indian Ocean. Because tsunamis travel and build so quickly, there was little warning—and the devastation was widespread.

△ A man searches among the wreckage on a beach in Phuket, Thailand, after a tsunami struck in December 2004. The massive wave was caused by an undersea earthquake.

When an earthquake occurs, the tension, or energy, is released as a series of seismic waves. These waves cause the destruction usually associated with earthquakes. The first waves to arrive are called "P" waves. These travel upward through Earth's crust at nearly 15,500 miles (25,000 km) per hour, but it is the slower "S" waves that generally cause more damage. The movement in these "S" waves is horizontal rather than vertical: they shake the ground sideways. Buildings and roads are more easily damaged by horizontal than vertical movement.

The effects of earthquakes

Primary effects of an earthquake happen immediately. The collapse of buildings is a primary effect because it happens immediately. Other effects cause problems over a longer period of time and are called secondary effects. A secondary effect is homelessness, as finding new housing will take time.

The amount of damage caused by an earthquake, and the number of people killed or injured, will vary from one earthquake to another. This is due to a number of factors:

The location of the focus: If this is near the surface, the earthquake is likely to cause more damage.
The location of the earthquake: If it hits a city, more damage will likely be caused and more people will be killed than if it hits in the countryside.
The country in which an earthquake occurs: The effects of earthquakes are usually much greater in poor countries. Buildings are generally less able to cope with earthquakes, and poor countries often have to wait for international aid.
The time of day: If an earthquake happens at night, most people will be asleep. They will not be able to evacuate buildings in time, so more people will be killed or injured.
The number of smaller earthquakes that follow the main one as the ground settles: These are called aftershocks and can cause great damage to already weakened buildings.

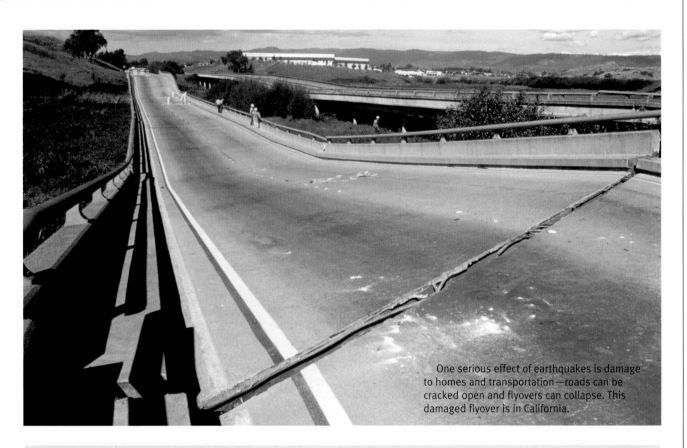

One serious effect of earthquakes is damage to homes and transportation—roads can be cracked open and flyovers can collapse. This damaged flyover is in California.

🌐 The earthquake that destroyed Bam

The city of Bam in southeast Iran lies near the boundary between the Iranian and Indian plates. The region is frequently hit by earthquakes. On the morning of December 26, 2003, an earthquake measuring 6.6 on the Richter scale devastated the city, destroying 80 percent of the buildings, including a fortress that had stood for more than 2,000 years. Some slight earth tremors had been felt the previous day, but this is not unusual for the region, so people took little notice. The first earthquake was still only minor and did not cause much damage. However, in the early hours of the morning, the second and stronger earthquake struck. Its epicenter was at the southern edge of the city of Bam. More than 26,000 of the city's 120,000 people were killed in the earthquake. It is estimated that the long-term cost of repairing the damage caused by the Bam earthquake will be nearly $2 billion.

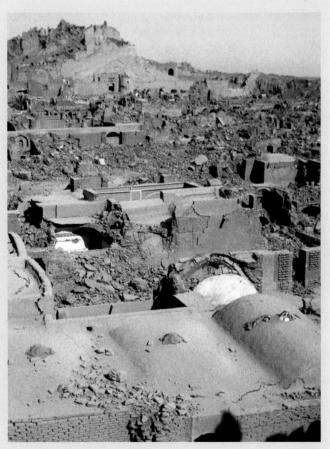

▷ The city of Bam in Iran was reduced to rubble by an earthquake in December 2003.

Earthquakes in the British Isles

The British Isles do not lie on the boundary between two plates, so they do not experience major earthquakes. It is not true, however, to say that there are never earthquakes in the British Isles. Any movement in Earth's crust, even if it is slight, can cause an earthquake. Unlike earthquakes concentrated on plate boundaries, those in the British Isles are widely scattered. The map shows the location of the earthquakes recorded in the 20th century. The biggest of these happened in 1931, at Dogger Bank in the North Sea. This earthquake measured 6.1 on the Richter scale.

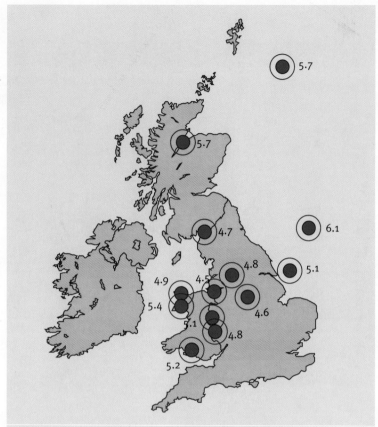

▶ The location and magnitude of earthquakes that hit the British Isles in the 20th century.

▲ Mount Vesuvius was responsible for burying the city of Pompeii in Italy in A.D. 79. Vesuvius is dormant but may erupt again one day.

▶▶ Mount Etna is the most active volcano in Europe. Here, a great column of ash rises above the mountain during the most explosive volcanic eruption of the last century.

Volcanic eruptions

A volcano is formed when magma from the mantle rises up through cracks in Earth's crust and erupts onto the surface. Above the surface, the magma solidifies and is called lava. Like earthquakes, most volcanic eruptions take place at or near the boundaries of plates. They are natural events and only become hazards to people when they erupt near areas of human settlement.

Many of the world's volcanoes have erupted recently and may do so again in the near future. These are called active volcanoes. Mount Etna in Italy is the most active volcano in Europe. Some volcanoes have not erupted for hundreds of years but may still erupt again in the future. These volcanoes, such as Vesuvius in Italy, are called dormant volcanoes. The third type of volcanoes are extinct volcanoes; they will never erupt again. The area of Le Puy in France is characterized by extinct volcanoes, which are being gradually worn away.

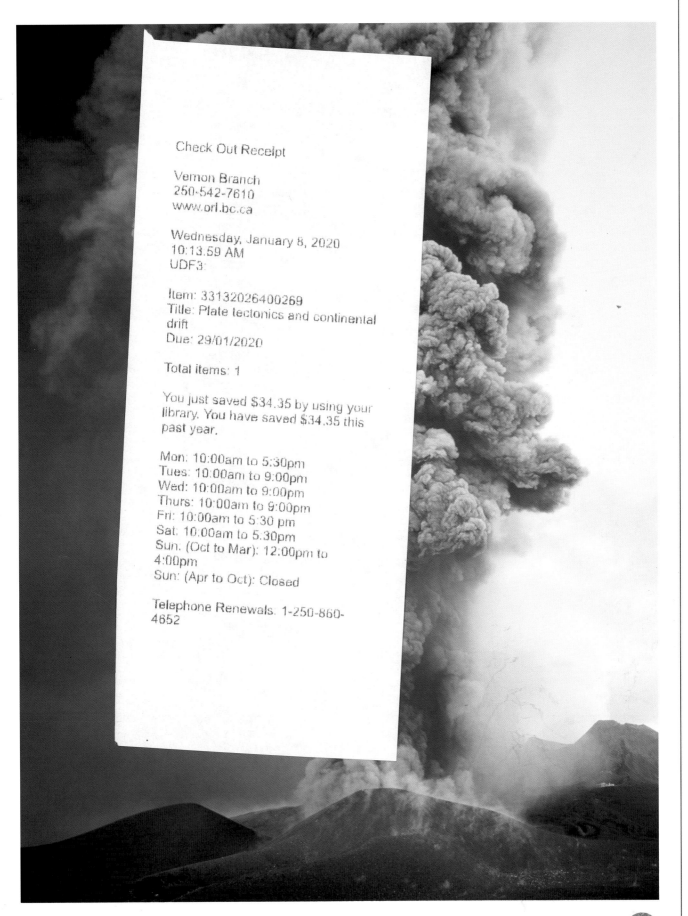

Check Out Receipt

Vernon Branch
250-542-7610
www.orl.bc.ca

Wednesday, January 8, 2020
10:13.59 AM
UDF3:

Item: 33132026400269
Title: Plate tectonics and continental drift
Due: 29/01/2020

Total items: 1

You just saved $34.35 by using your library. You have saved $34.35 this past year.

Mon: 10:00am to 5:30pm
Tues: 10:00am to 9:00pm
Wed: 10:00am to 9:00pm
Thurs: 10:00am to 9:00pm
Fri: 10:00am to 5:30 pm
Sat: 10:00am to 5.30pm
Sun. (Oct to Mar): 12:00pm to 4:00pm
Sun: (Apr to Oct): Closed

Telephone Renewals. 1-250-860-4652

A composite volcano.

A shield volcano.

Types of volcanoes

Not all volcanoes are exactly the same. Their size and shape depend mainly on the type of magma in an eruption. The most common types of volcanoes are composite, shield, and caldera volcanoes.

Some of the world's most spectacular and beautiful mountains are composite volcanoes. Magma rises to Earth's surface through a central vent; the volcano may also have secondary or smaller vents. The volcano grows in size as eruptions pour more lava onto the surface, along with dust and ash. Composite volcanoes are usually very steep-sided, such as Mount Fuji in Japan.

Shield volcanoes are built up from huge and repeated lava flows. The lava erupts slowly and spreads over a wide area.

The Soufriere Hills volcano, Montserrat

Montserrat is an island in the Caribbean Sea. It is part of the island arc formed where the Caribbean plate is colliding with the North and South American plates. After hundreds of years as a dormant volcano, the composite Soufriere Hills volcano on Montserrat erupted in 1997. Eruptions of the volcano continued for several months, until December 26, when the top of the volcano collapsed. A cloud of ash and dust was thrown 16,400 feet (5,000 m) into the atmosphere. Nineteen people were killed in the main eruptions, and the whole island was covered in a thick layer of ash. The volcano continues to show signs of activity, but these are at a low level and are carefully monitored.

▶ Thick clouds of steam and ash billowing from the Soufriere Hills volcano.

Some of the largest volcanoes in the world are shield volcanoes. The Hawaiian islands are made of a series of shield volcanoes. The largest of these, Mauna Loa, reaches more than 13,100 feet (4,000 m) above sea level. Mauna Loa is more than 29,500 feet (9,000 m) in height—another 16,400 feet (5,000 m) of the volcano is hidden below sea level. Surtsey, in Iceland, is another example of a shield volcano.

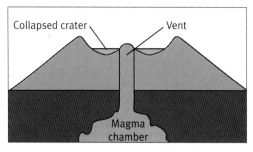

▲ A caldera volcano.

The largest and most violent volcanic eruptions come from caldera volcanoes. They hurl hundreds of cubic miles of magma onto Earth's surface. When so much magma is suddenly removed from under a volcano, the ground collapses, and the whole summit of the volcano is blown away, forming a huge hollow called a caldera. Some calderas are several miles in width and depth and often contain lakes or have been flooded by the sea. Krakatoa in Indonesia is an example of a caldera volcano.

🌑 Volcano damage

Lava flows destroy anything in their paths. Scientists have tried various methods of stopping or redirecting them but have had little success. The most violent eruptions explode fragments of rock out of a volcano. These rocks travel down the sides of a volcano at speeds of more than 90 miles (150 km) per hour. Most of the 30,000 people killed when Mount Pelée in Martinique erupted in 1902 were killed by these pyroclastic flows. Clouds of dust and ash fall after explosive eruptions. This dust can ruin crops, damage transportation and communications, and be harmful to people's health. The dust and ash may rise high into the atmosphere and block some of the sun's rays.

▶ When Mount Pinatubo in the Philippines erupted in 1991, it hurled 22 million tons (20 million t) of material into the atmosphere. This circled the globe and reduced temperatures around the world by 1.8 °F (1 °C).

Glossary

active volcano A volcano that erupts regularly, at any time.

aftershocks Earthquake waves that occur after the main earthquake.

caldera A large volcanic crater formed by the collapse of a volcano's cone during a very explosive eruption.

composite volcano A volcano made of alternate layers of ash and lava; it may have side (subsidiary) vents and cones.

continental crust Parts of Earth's crust made of light rocks. They are made of compounds containing silica (sand) and aluminum.

continental drift The theory by Alfred Wegener that explains why Earth's continents appear to move and split into different sections.

convection current A current of hot magma in the mantle. It rises from the lower part of the mantle, where temperatures are hottest, toward the crust.

convergent boundary A boundary at which two plates are moving toward each other. The denser plate dips below the other and melts.

core The central section of Earth; the inner core is solid, and the outer core is molten.

crust The surface, or outer layer, of Earth.

crystalline rocks Rocks containing crystals, including quartz and feldspar.

divergent boundary Where two or more plates are moving apart, often resulting in mid-ocean ridges and volcanic islands; also called a constructive boundary.

dormant volcano A volcano that has not recently erupted but may do so again.

earthquake A sudden and often violent movement caused by release of pressure in rocks deep below Earth's surface.

epicenter The point on Earth's surface vertically above the focus, where the worst damage usually occurs in an earthquake.

extinct volcano A volcano that no longer erupts.

fault A fracture in Earth's crust caused by the movement of plates at transform boundaries; earthquakes are frequent occurrences along faults.

focus The point underground from which an earthquake originates.

fold mountains Mountains made of a set of parallel ridges caused when the continental rocks pile up at a destructive boundary or collision zone.

fossil The compacted and hardened remains of plants or creatures that died millions of years ago.

geothermal energy Energy derived from natural underground heat in rocks.

Gondwanaland A continent formed after the split of the original super-continent of Pangaea, comprised of Africa, Australia, South America, and Antarctica.

hot spot An area on Earth's surface where the crust is very thin. Magma can break through and form a volcano.

inner core The solid inner part of the central section of Earth.

intraplate A point within a plate not near its edges.

island arc A chain of islands formed when volcanoes created on the ocean floor grow tall enough to break the surface.

Laurasia A continent formed after the split of the original super-continent of Pangaea, comprised of Europe, Asia, and North America.

lava Magma that erupts onto the surface of Earth through a vent or fissure in a volcano.

leading edge The edge of a plate that is farthest away from the adjoining plate; the leading edge is made up of the oldest rock.

lithosphere The solid outer layer of Earth, from the Greek *lithos*, meaning "stone."

magma Molten rock present beneath Earth's surface.

magnitude The amount of energy released in an earthquake.

mantle The layer of Earth above the core and beneath the crust.

Mid-Atlantic Ridge The name given to the mid-ocean ridge stretching down the center of the Atlantic Ocean.

mid-ocean ridges Zones on the ocean floor where oceanic plates are moving apart and new crust is created.

natural disaster Something likely to result in loss of life or damage to property that is not caused by people.

ocean trenches Deep oceanic areas where one plate is dragged beneath another.

oceanic crust The thinnest and youngest parts of Earth's crust, largely made up of the dense rock basalt.

outer core The molten outer part of the central section of Earth.

P waves Primary or "push" waves; earthquake waves that travel from the epicenter up to the surface of Earth.

Pangaea Earth's original super-continent, in which all of the present continents formed one huge land mass.

Panthalassa Earth's original single ocean surrounding the super-continent of Pangaea.

plate boundary zone A broad region where two or more plates meet but where the exact boundaries are not certain.

plate tectonics The theory developed in the 1960s from earlier ideas of continental drift. It explains the nature of Earth's plates, the way they move, and the features that form at their boundaries, including earthquakes and volcanoes.

plates The moving slabs of rock that make up Earth's crust. There are nine large plates and several smaller ones.

primary effects The immediate effects of an earthquake.

pyroclastic flow Volcanic ash, dust, bombs, and other fragments in hot, dense gases, which roll downhill at high speeds.

Richter scale A scale for measuring the energy, or magnitude, of an earthquake.

rift A valley formed when a plate cracks in the middle of a continent.

S waves Secondary or "shake" waves; earthquake waves that travel away from the epicenter.

seafloor spreading The renewal of Earth's crust, formed by magma bubbling up through the mantle, then cooling and hardening on contact with the ocean.

secondary effects The long-term effects of an earthquake.

sedimentary rock A type of rock formed from sediment that is compressed over time until it becomes solid.

seismic waves Movements in Earth's crust that indicate that an earthquake may be about to happen or is already happening.

seismologist A scientist or geologist who studies earthquakes.

shield volcano A broad volcano built up by large and repeated lava flows.

subduction zone A destructive plate boundary where a dense oceanic plate is forced below a lighter continental one, where it melts.

trailing edge The edge of a plate closest to the adjoining plate; new crust is constantly being formed at the trailing edge of plates, and it is therefore made up of the youngest rock.

transform boundary Where two or more plates slide horizontally past each other; also known as a conservative boundary.

tremor A mild shaking on the surface of Earth, usually an indication that an earthquake is about to occur.

trench-flipping The sudden reversal of subduction when an oceanic and continental plate meet.

tsunami A large wave caused by an undersea earthquake or volcanic eruption.

vent The hollow, central part of a volcano, out of which lava, steam, and other materials are ejected.

volcanic eruption The emission of solid, liquid, and gaseous material from a volcano.

volcano A crack in Earth's crust, through which molten rock, gases, ash, and dust erupt.

weathering The wearing away of rock by rain, frost, plant roots, and burrowing animals.

zone of activity An area within which earthquakes or volcanic eruptions are likely to take place.

Further Information

Books

Englebert, Phillis. *Dangerous Planet: The Science of Natural Disasters*. Detroit: UXL, 2001.

Gallant, Roy A. *Dance of the Continents*. New York: Benchmark Books, 2000.

Oxlade, Chris. *Earth's Changing Landscapes: Earthquakes & Volcanoes*. North Mankato, Minn.: Smart Apple Media, 2005

Vogel, Carole Garbuny. *Shifting Shores*. New York: Franklin Watts, 2003.

Walsh Shepherd, Donna. *Earth*. New York: Franklin Watts, 2002.

Web sites

http://www.enchantedlearning.com/subjects/ astronomy/planets/earth/Continents
A colorful site with maps and text explaining how tectonic plates work.

http://www.extremescience.com/Plate Tectonicsmap.htm
Learn more about the boundaries between plates through illustrations and a map that shows the layout of Earth's tectonic plates.

http://www.platetectonics.com
A fascinating site with many articles and links providing information about how our planet is in constant change.

http://volcano.und.nodak.edu/vwdocs/ vwlessons/plate_tectonics/introduction.html
A Web site that explains the geographical evolution of Earth, including fossil information, rock sequences, and glaciation.

http://www.usgs.gov/
Home page of the U.S. Geological Survey, with resources and new stories about the geography and geology of the United States, including information and updates about earthquakes and volcanoes.

Index

Acknowledgements

Picture Credits

Cover: (t) US Geological Survey/Science Photo Library
(bl) © Pierre Vauthey/Corbis Sygma (br) Bernhard Edmaier/
Science Photo Library 6 Bernhard Edmaier/Science Photo
Library 7 Dr Ken MacDonald/Science Photo Library
11(t) Planetary Visions Ltd/Science Photo Library 11(b) Science
Photo Library 12 Bernhard Edmaier/Science Photo Library
15 © Pierre Vauthey/Corbis Sygma 18(t) © Jonathan
Blair/Corbis 19 J. P. Danvoye, Publiphoto Diffusion/ Science
Photo Library 20(t) B. Murton/Southampton Oceanography
Centre/Science Photo Library 20(b) Institute of Oceanographic
Sciences/NERC/Science Photo Library 22 © Ralph White/
Corbis 23(b) Will & Den McIntyre/Science Photo Library
24 W. Haxby, Lamont-Doherty Earth Observatory/Science Photo
Library 25(b) US Geological Survey/Science Photo Library
26(t) NASA/Science Photo Library 27(t) Simon Fraser/Science
Photo Library 28(r) © Roger Ressmeyer/ Corbis 29(b) Peter
Menzel/Science Photo Library 30(t) © Roger Ressmeyer/Corbis
30(b) © Wolfgang Kaehler/Corbis 31 US Geological Survey/
Science Photo Library 32(t) G. Brad Lewis/Science Photo
Library 32(b) NASA/Science Photo Library 33 Stephen &
Donna O'Meara/Science Photo Library 36 © Luis Ascui/
Reuters/Corbis 37(t) Ed Young/Science Photo Library
37(b) © Shahpari Sohale/Corbis 38(b) Mauro Fermariello/
Science Photo Library 39 Bernhard Edmaier/Science Photo
Library 40(b) Stephen & Donna O'Meara/Science Photo
Library 41(b) Robert M. Carey, NOAA/Science Photo Library